Here Comes the Sun

Written by Amanda Graham
Illustrated by Greg Holfeld

Here comes the sun.
Shimmer,
shine.

Here comes the wind.
Shiver,
shake.

Here comes the storm.
Flash,
crash.

Here comes the rain.
Splish,
splash.

9

Sheep in the mud.
Slush,

mush.

Run to the shop.
Rush,
dash.

Put on the coats.
Put on the hats.
Put on the socks.
Put on the boots.

Oh no!
Here comes the sun.

Shimmer,
shine.

16